FLOAT

FLOAT

David Abel

chax
2012

Many thanks to the editors of magazines in which excerpts from "Orbis Pictus" first appeared: *26* (Joseph Noble & Avery Burns), *New Ohio Review* (Catherine Taylor), and *Take Out* (Laura Winter).

Sources, dates of composition, and related information can be found in the notes beginning on page 137.

ISBN 978 0 925904 29 4

Chax Press
411 N 7th Avenue Suite 103
Tucson Arizona 85705-8388
USA

for Franz Kamin
(1941–2010)

When there is nothing left,
it is the time for giving gifts

"Statements on Doing Nothing"

CONDUCTION

How is a puppet like a landscape?

(which is, by definition, an *image*)

I blame equally those who take on themselves to praise, and those who take on themselves to blame, and those who merely amuse themselves, and I can only approve of those who seek with tears . . . [BG]

The gesture — hand raised high, two fingers extended in a "V," eyes never lifting from the book in his hand — of a dark-skinned *joven* in white clothing, leaning back against a pole by the side of the highway, strikes and passes through me, as though I were for that instant the consciousness of the environment, registering a passing wave, in its limitless demonstrations . . .

Scientific instruments can lack accuracy, but they must be able to distinguish between phenomena . . . No one has thus far been able to define a notion like "complexity" sufficiently well that we could someday hope to build a complexity detector. [JL1]

Just as aperiodic rhythm can include periodic rhythm, just as process can include object, so free improvisations can include strict ones, can even include compositions. [JC1]

13

Struggling to escape, again and again, every day because it begins with the return of the undreamed, the noose of rationality, as though on a treadmill

tonight's eclipse a sign and a warrant

and every shadow nostalgia for an invisible interior

I am interested in relinquishing control . . . and I think "chaos" is terrifying and so for me it takes courage to draw it . . . in fact, I am trying to overcome my fear of it. [AH1]

Un ciego estaba escribiendo
lo que el mudo le decia
y un sordo estaba escuchando
para contarlo al otro dia. [FT]

A blind man was writing
what the mute would say
and a deaf man was listening
so he could tell it another day.

To make a prairie it takes a clover and one bee,
One clover, and a bee,
And revery.
The revery alone will do,
If bees are few. [ED]

To Rauschenberg is owed much of the basic cultural
assumption that a work of art can exist for any length of
time, in any material . . . anywhere . . . for any purpose . . .
and any destination it chooses . . . [RH]

The meaning of a meaning
(its tendency)

is more than the sum, sequence, or
description

of its instances

The faculty of sight developed as an active response to
continually changing contingencies. [JB]

Quick Study

Federal income tax
stain removal

bar guide
chef's math

Shakespeare and his times

The "mystery" — of seeing at all, of memory — is evoked, when we thought it had been exhausted . . . and if there are no "memories" (in the sense of *objects*), rather only a process of reenactment — then a symbol of a reenactment (its "objects" also phantoms) . . .

walls, fences
we can only decorate
florid in speech or
hysterical

the dictionary is
purple
because it is
incomplete

(where "purple" stands for
"beautiful, lovely, mute")

the most exhaustive work
is exceeded the moment
eyes lay on it

yet it remains
they remain
I remain
we remain

Of course such lists are not only *not* comprehensive, they are artifacts of the backward glance.

Yet, like Lot's wife, we can't resist. Just as we can hardly resist writing, making art, our profundities, our excavations, which are nothing if not our graves.

My medium is:

> traffic
> congestion
> sprawl
> etcetera

I sculpt human error — failure — bad faith —
ill intent — etcetera

*And it became evident that metaphor was not just pretty
poetry, it was not either good or bad logic, but was in fact
the logic upon which the biological world had been built,
the main characteristic and organizing glue of this world of
mental process which I have been trying to sketch for you in
some way or another . . . I hope it may have done something
to set you free from thinking in material and logical terms,
in the syntax and terminology of mechanics, when you are in
fact trying to think about living things.* [GB]

Hinting that an element of data should be cached in a
temporal structure implies that it is likely to be read in the
near future.

I imagine Franz Kamin handing Nick Bantock a puzzle
after a book signing by the latter, then disappearing —
Bantock can't solve it, no matter how hard he tries;
seeks expert assistance to no avail, becomes obsessed:
can't discover who Franz is nor find him again, thus

"performing" Franz's composition — both of them write about the experience, in their disparate styles (raw/cooked).

Computers have been given the ontological kid glove treatment. Relativity is necessary to explain the observed universe, while computer science is not. [JL1]

As to the 'great painting,' its beautiful white panel is always on the wall before me, and I am thinking great things into it. I have thought so many beautiful things into it that it ought to make a great print just as it is . . . [MP]

Recently someone carried out an odd project: to count how many notes Schubert wrote. Perhaps his energy was somewhat misplaced. He arrived at a horrifying number and asked the following question: "Leaving aside genius, how much time would it take simply to write this number of notes?" After investigating the matter, he found that it would take about twenty-five years. Well, Schubert only took fifteen years to put millions of notes on paper. Where did this power come from? [NB]

In terms of the language of "display," a collection is a very powerful unit . . . artists sidestep "content" by creating a self-contained mode of display . . . repetition is very powerful, but it is useless if the content doesn't require it. [AH1]

surveillance as vampirism
endless prelude

kinship of fringes

"work is its own cure"
and I'm incurable

*GORPLE: the semiconscious activity comprising tiny
repetitious movements which may portend contact with that
miasmic subcosm in which miniscule vermicular messages are
located and found to be so interlinked as to be unintelligible
to most.* [FK1]

*Because the faculty of sight is continuous, because the visual
categories (red, yellow, dark, thick, thin) remain constant,
and because so many things appear to remain in place,
one tends to forget that the visual is always the result of
an unrepeatable, momentary encounter. Appearances, at
any given moment, are a construction from the debris of
everything which has previously appeared.* [JB]

Manager: Remember, it's soft wood you're splitting . . .

Poet: Go find yourself some other slave! . . .

Comedian: Nothing will satisfy a finished taste . . .

Poet: I had nothing, yet enough . . .

Manager: What good is talking about inspiration? [JG]

I really feel sorry for people who think things like soap dishes or mirrors or Coke bottles are ugly, because they're surrounded by things like that all day long, and it must make them miserable . . . If you don't change your mind about something when you confront a picture you've not seen before, either you're a stubborn fool or the painting is not very good. [RR]

I've been spending most of my afternoons walking around urban residential neighborhoods, documenting the wiring and ventilation systems . . . wires and pipes drape with wild abandon over the rooftops and make their way into buildings via any possible architectural orifice. Often windows are simply broken . . . despite the harsh winters . . . it both delights and terrifies me. [AH1]

The sitting evokes something of planetary movement, something of the dance . . . I glimpse the possibility of working out the music to this dance. For any given work of sculpture one could find a corresponding piece of music, created to the rhythms of the sculptor's actions. [PV]

Is the world full? or is Creation incomplete?

Which is more fleeting:

a passage of music,

or the physical circumstances of any life at a given moment

(e.g., the dirt on my floor)?

A large man in a Denver Broncos coat walks out —
a teen walks into La Gran Café de la Parroquia and bares
her navel to the room, pulling back her hair — a man at
the next table in his fifties or sixties has the hair pattern,
moustache, and cyclopean sight of my father, and his
inwardness — I don't expect to solve any mysteries,
puzzles, here — or anywhere.

The Pacific giant octopus is by far the largest of all octopus
and the biggest-brained of all invertebrates. It may reach
twenty feet or more (tentacle to tentacle) in its tragically
short life — before it mates, once, when it is three to five
years old, and dies.

My old catch-phrase:

Information is Alienated Experience. [JL1]

this deepening
has its dawn
beyond any
masquerade

any mask I am,
even the pretense
of words
such as these

we meet by
the fountain
or flash,
electric

across each other's
eyes, hoping
for a natural
symbol

a sky
that leaves us
equally,
sinking

*It is astonishing: the moment, here in a wink, gone in a
wink, nothing before and nothing after, returns nevertheless
as a spectre to disturb the calm of a later moment . . .* [FN]

Thinking about writing about having read what I wrote
at some long-past moment — and not having access now
to what was implied and (crucially) then adjacent — a
"link," the loss of which transforms the actual function of
the artifact that remains.

Bernhard's "Venus Comb" (1943) — I thought about
buying one in Veracruz. Would I have looked at it like she
has? Could I have?

I do like objects, but I need other people to *see* them for
me. What would that *not* be true for?

Well, I see their images . . .

Much of his prose is involved with the delineation of
sensibility in its experience of time: what happens, and
how often, if at all? what does each second mean, and how
is the span of attention used to make it a longer or shorter
experience? is Time in itself beautiful, or is its quality merely
decorable or decorous? Somehow, he gives an equation in
which attention equals Life, or is its only evidence . . . [OH]

Some recent speculation concerned with "Complexity" . . .
suggests that forms in the universe are limited to a far smaller
variety than we might have thought . . . even if this turns out
to be right . . . a limited variety of territories does not imply a
limited number of maps. [JL1]

Lonely bones can't sleep nights. Singing
insects keep calling them, calling them.

And the old have no tears. When they sob,
autumn weeps dewdrops. Strength failing

all at once, as if cut loose, and ravages
everywhere, like weaving unraveled,

I touch thread-ends. No new feelings.
Memories crowding thickening sorrow,

how could I bear southbound sails, how
wander rivers and mountains of the past? [MC]

Without consciousness, the universe would be exactly the same, in terms of what its particles would be doing. A camera placed in a consciousness-free universe would record exactly the same scene. The same photons would travel the same courses through the lens . . . the particles of a piece of wood would be in just the same locations at the same moment, but the notion that the collection of particles is also a piece of wood would not be put forward . . . [JL2]

The present moment is not a precise point but a messy approximation, fraught with compromise and illusion . . . however, while consciousness cannot distinguish the present moment with consistency or precision, there is no other candidate in a deterministic universe that can distinguish it at all. [JL2]

And then there's Tintoretto's aphorism:

"Good colors aren't bought on the Rialto!"

I simply couldn't buy genius. [NB]

A combination of characteristics: dense, vibrant rhythm within constrained compass (thus the pattern *almost* parsable) — as in moving water . . .

Rauschenberg's esthetic of the unrepeatable glance, the second time you look, the work has changed, is connected to the kind of instantaneous overall perception clarified later by a vastly different kind of art. But once the Rauschenberg work broke down, that is, on the second glance, it lapsed into a kind of additive dementia. The only time it held together was at first glance. It takes years to put it together again for the museum audience, and of course the past decade has more or less accomplished that.

Works such as Rauschenberg's thus have a lost mode of perception buried in them, as the esthetic of "museum perception" instructs academic modes of looking quite alien to the original. [OD]

Of course, human beings are the medium that flows through the conduits of environment and edifice — always shaped space — and yet the structures (material and conceptual) are equally extensions, projections, enacted and sustained by a tendency within that very flow.

Something of what we are actually permeates the physical world — and vice versa. There is a (pataphysical) chemistry that explains these interactions at a deep level — a polymer physics of the encounter, the marriage of matter and spirit.

. . . to a Martian, a Macintosh is the same sort of thing as a toaster or a rock. In order to perceive information, you have to put it in a cultural context, and that re-opens the can of worms that zombies have been trying to solder shut. Could "information" just be a shell game that hides the nut of old-style consciousness? [JL1]

*I'm not saying these bees are kittens, but they can be worked
with.* [RM]

False Echo

The City of Sadness
     extended
  in all directions

          as though they were pockets,
     migration
          out of season is a product

of the point of view
of an eye no longer
          practiced

in the true illusions.
Electric, our temperaments are modulated
before we know
     whether the strings are in tune
     or even still there.

But you
have preserved your method
against its own success, distress.

That it keeps you,
unconsoled
     company
out of habit intuited
  between spasms

     and how that too must change
     inside gratitude,
     for example

The future is reaching back and holding apart the strands of barbed wire . . .

. . . it was pleasant to see a pile of tangled wool in her knitting basket fighting a losing battle for a few hours to retain its shape . . . [JC2]

David —
more bits for your perusal.
the photos are the subjects for the puzzles . . .

Just returned from an amazing road trip. Am off to China tomorrow. What a crazy life . . .

PS Also firefly piece. look at that foot! [AH2]

"Natural forms" — does the *drama* inhere in the ontic? — we say that the artist elicits it — but — the *mutability* — must precede the fuss of the artist (of the human?)

The string of numbers that runs a particular computer has to perfectly follow the rules of that computer or the computer will crash. But if you can find the matching computer, any particular string of numbers can run a program . . . If your brain is functionally equivalent to a computer program, there is no reason a meteor shower can't be that program, if you take the trouble to find the right computer to run it. [JL1]

but think about it, she said, everybody is glad to have a roof even if it's ugly, and evenings, on the way home past the hospital grounds, there is always a double bass leaning in the second floor window [FM]

Social insects, in their division of labor . . . can be thought of as a supraorganism or as a massing of small individual parts. When viewed in its detail, a hive is full of motion and transition . . . and when viewed as a supraorganism the hive operates as a cohesive and ordered unit. [AH1]

Dr. Morse was a quiet man of fluid motion . . . He had figured out a way to lure swarms of bees to follow him wherever he walked. [RM]

We are at the top of a pyramid, the peak of a mountain that is *rising* (even as material constantly washes and blows away, it grows) — in fifty years there will be a hundred cities as large as this. This is the future, not the past.

"See what this looks like; even a child knows this, until they make him forget. When a certain level of saturation is achieved then it is in a prepared state for entrainment." The whole page was covered with scribbles . . . "Vibratory systems entrain each other . . . If you go to a pond at dusk, you'll hear

the frogs start to sing a few at a time. Eventually, as it grows darker, all the frogs will be singing in a mass chaotic chorus. Within an hour they'll all be in syncopation . . . it always happens." He tapped the scribbled paper with the eraser of the pencil. Something went wrong with my eyes for a moment: the scribbling seemed to straighten itself out into a clearly defined complex pattern. I shook my head. "Uh-huh," he said, "Well, 'ventually you'll get it." [FK2]

Description describes describing means

    or

Measurement describes the instrument; and

Description describes the mind

I almost never taste. I eat a meal while giving a lesson and I don't notice what I eat. And then suddenly there's something extraordinary, a peach . . . Two years ago, I had a cherry that was a masterpiece of a cherry. From time to time I think of it. I've never eaten its equal. [NB]

When I'm gone, I just *was,* that's all. That is, I was just "like so" — these clothes, these discrepancies. This effort, not another.

The Copenhagen interpretation of quantum mechanics
says that the universe must be split into two parts, each of
which is governed by very different laws. Above the split is
the real world . . . Below the split the laws are different.
No observations are allowed . . . on the critical question of
where must the split be placed, Von Neumann came up
with the most amazing answer: IT CAN BE PLACED
ANYWHERE . . . [SK]

You nougat-cooker.

You donkey-fireman, you doffer,
you cube-cutting-machine dumper.

You cigar-box repairman.

ORBIS PICTUS

One might say that the world is hardly more ancient than the art of making the world . . .

in any case our idea of the origin of things is never more than a reverie based on their present disposition . . .

the cosmogonic form . . . includes sacred books, admirable poems, outlandish narratives full of beauties and absurdities, and physico-mathematical researches often so profound as to be worthy of a less insignificant subject than the universe. But it is the glory of the species, and something more than their glory, to waste their powers on the void.

Paul Valéry

Land Sought, Found, Claimed

Underneath these humanistic, these secular ideas, there is an alchemical activity going on in the plant kingdom, in the mineral kingdom, as if the leaves on the trees just come out in the spring because they love to, as if rubies and emeralds grow in the rocks like drops of intense love, as if the rocks themselves are full of desire, reaching toward some crystalline intensity, some luminosity inside themselves.

James Hillman

Ditto . . . conceived in the fiery bowels, born in the midst of sudden eruptions "past consensuses are no longer seen as viable." After years of travail they have taken according to the laws of nature, under tremendous pressure. "Worlds differ in the relevant kinds they comprise." The trajectory is one that grows increasingly 'increasingly melancholy' melancholy. "Natural" is an inapt term to cover not only biological species but such artificial kinds as musical works, psychological experiments, and types of machinery *an octave is a cave* when the places of discovery *I thought I'd done* in the midst of the ordinary stone we may at any moment come upon some absolute categorical or psychological priority difficult to get at or detach having points as certain classes of nesting volumes or having points as certain pairs of intersecting lines or as certain triples of intersecting planes gleaming like stars in the dark . . . modern technics for turning over and sifting the near-famous, for driving galleries in, sometimes, in more lavish mood, the mountain torrents wash away passionate card-players or a landslide carries them down into a valley where they will then lie embedded in boulders or rubble. *Supply the latest machines.* In the summer of 1831 an exceptional hurricane sweeping through the eastern valleys of the Ural Mountains uprooted a giant tree *a direct quote*. The next morning some peasants who had come to gape at fallen majesty noticed that they were no more than raw material whose worth was determined by the cost of production and the functional value they possessed as supplying the needs of present-day technology, and could never be "proof against chemical and mechanical attacks."

Acknowledged as taking anything I can add *I plate* interior
I plate one invincible fragment of eternity composed
of another already on hand dissolved into function
"substance dissolved" made from other versions. It differs
from common pencil lead.

that proclaim it king derive from nothing else but this
peculiar

The scrap has for years gone on being forcibly pushed up
from the interior towards the outer crust, as in the case of
the Great Mogul and the immaculately white

They cut down into the blue earth

In the flowery language of the East, a drop of the heart's blood is derived from one to two percent of the Latin, to which it owes July. According to ancient legends, Earth is the red of pigeon's blood. *They float*

Those of the correctest color are found embedded in snow-white chalk. Next in rank come the dark, sometimes even brownish. To be considered perfect, not only the right shade but brilliant and pure (the latter is the rarest, almost always tiny secondary so-called needles come into existence). Often there will also be faint wisps caused by tiny drops of moisture but these are actually a part of the idiosyncrasy and mysterious beauty.

Pedro the Cruel invaded the Middle Ages in 1367. It has nevertheless retained its old name, since it was presented to the Black Prince. He was sort of a cutout of the old into the new design. This is well illustrated in a little book he wrote about farmers.

Well it, at least this, doesn't

It must be getting close *without modifications*

After four straight years traced back to various families
of languages, the most coveted glorious velvety deep inky
flossy finest mysterious fateful favorite pell-mell absolute
negotiated same

Due to foreign elements varying according to the
proportion of recent research under favorable conditions
shining through a red envelope (*see article in centerfold*)
getting close to watching light-reflecting comprisals float
like an astral body my television myself free thank you

to bring peace to the soul, to exhort to fidelity and to keep
away feelings of hate, sometimes also in Australia

new "wholehearted" helicopters, the rings of cardinals and
bishops

Their name was derived from the Sanscrit but is now used for all of the same class. They vary greatly in color and have been called, since delicate shades are frequent, and have names of their own, reflexes caused by dense groupings, so the student can not only distinguish the real from the false but can tell one from another and in many cases even determine the place of extraction from a study of the inclusions. The Chinese used foreign bodies to cover metal cords and fixed these to the bow of a saw. Three intersecting directions produce three intersecting lines of light. Remnants of plants or insects give them the stamp of individual personalities.

Fairy landscapes, glimmering submarine worlds, enchanted gardens, grotesque figures, fantastic castles form a kind of microcosm full of information about the great pine forests of the North. Pliny speaks of this phenomenon with the utmost amazement.

The prime source of the Pharaohs' wealth goes back to the Spanish conquistadores Cortés and Pizarro who brought back to Europe in the sixteenth century the cool depths of the sea when the sky is clear and the sun shines brightly. A royal hand we admire was exploited by the Indians before the Spanish Conquest. They called it Somondoco. The subtle, mysterious "jardin" is hardly ever clear but in it the inclusions form an additional beauty.

History: Julius Caesar, now in America, nearly five inches high.

Fable: A little jug, known to the ancient Egyptians, seeing in it an emblem of hope and a reminder of fresh spring green.

The name of Alexander is given to one of the most
mysterious families. Christened after Czar Alexander II
because the first individual is supposed to have come
to light in Tokovaya in the Ural Mountains on the day
the Czar came of age in 1831, nowadays found only
in Ceylon, in considerably larger numbers. Their main
peculiarity is that they change color. They are particularly
valued by connoisseurs who will pay high prices for them.
It is to be regretted that other variants, among the finest
specimens, have not as yet won the recognition that they
deserve.

Quite different from the preceding, but equally strange, it
owes its name to a milky gleam that passes over its surface
because of the way light is reflected by fine-spun capillary
filaments lying embedded parallel to one another below
the surface. This moving strip of light creates the illusion
of a slit gliding over the rounded surface with the resulting
resemblance to the pupil of an eye.

Washed ashore from the sea where they had lain in the
sirens' caskets,

By appropriate heating changed, more acceptable, without
any trace being left of this artificial intervention,

Promising prosperous voyages, J. P. Morgan

If, however, extraneous elements enter

Special healing powers were ascribed to ancient myths.
In former times they were used as glasses for short-
sightedness. In the Middle Ages they also served as magic
mirrors in which to read the future.

Ambulatory Windows

The manufacture of wonder was an invention of the early alchemists.

It was shrouded in so much mystery that it gave rise to all sorts of glass.

glass   what is glass

glass is a solution
of sand and chalk and ashes
fused by fire
it is a desert
that transmits light

the thirst is not appeased

David Antin

Homo Faber . . . gazing up in wonder hardly suspecting the throes of the rent, Kali invoked walking up Second Avenue the funerary air Sundays in or out, lilac-toned ministries marking the beginning and the end of the spun intended. In the century that lay between such hereditary breakfast and the latest culinary wave hundreds of churches, simple village churches as well as great cathedrals enriched through wars symbolic of the faith of the Middle Ages. To all who emptied out of the vehicle, dead or not yet dead, presenting an unforgettable image of light, strength, and repose it offers warmth and security, the highest perfection, usually in the vernacular and markedly on market days and feasts.

In times when lust or grain was stronger than any feeling for stories, the old awe provided an incentive for inspiring and destroying the fables. Secrets of earlier ways of making manuscripts were revealed when an old monk, Theophilus, who lived in Germany lay down in his work at the beginning of the 12th century. Diverse arts were scheduled to come to light. Both material and method proved employment, perfectly said. One parted the sand bed of the river; two added a little common salt term to burn the bracken from the beechwood branch — this was all in flux, no one was red-hot for several hours. It is no accident that the chart became the center of the manufacture; they built themselves huts on the outs particularly fine clearing mixing in the veining.

gluttons and stableboys and a cordon of bedlam
mysterious realm of blown glass, failed uprights
amidst the gourmands that yield the city;
I'm counting on my bones   to be around   to erode

this drink is on the flag
all sequences have necks
having to do with the breaking
of reeds sense stretched around order

Lebanon

The motif is always the same: a female figure with a significant book. Bodies are the truest sense of words. The intention of the glossary is not simply to provide a guide to words and forms that do not occur; literary coexistence has proved a doubtful asset in the history of poetry. The decay movement has been unable to advance beyond Scotland in Monopoly. At least in part coterminous with their own vividness, the speakers like Latin, English, Arabic. Though its scent suffered a number that threw out backs, the various strongly marked disruptions followed themselves in reverse, left to themselves, radio.

Introduction

Open any book. Your good nature will bring you
unbounded happiness. It would probably not be possible
for human beings to perform this — Accept the next
proposition that you hear. To go back to the mountaintop.
Oh cold wind my hands forget everything. On the soft
and dirty rooves of the city, I forgot. I searched for what
was lost, in the lonely rooms of handsome strangers, in
the dreams of embarrassed immigrants, in the architect's
sky with its well-designed clouds . . .

I am haunted — by numbers that repeat, pursued by
mechanical darkness. Someone will come to tell this story:

A vine cluster. A lock of light. Hold on to the locks
of its hair. She curls the locks of my hair with her
fingers. When it comes to grow green. The leaves
were very green. A green dream. We have planted
the greens by the water of your spring. The green
shade. A green note. The green nights. Your green
eyes. The fire erases and eats away its greenness.
The most costly vegetables.

Open any book — close the first and open another. You
become the story. The book is only something lost, a
boy who died a child, the night crowded with vacancy.
Implacable stories. No number disappears; the lights
go out but the number three repeated three times, the
number one repeated four times, the number twelve
repeated twice — I turn the lights on and off by thinking
about the numbers.

Someone is sending me a message:

Care draws its lines with an iron nail.

Of what use to me are eyes that do not see you?

1.

O old nest,
my toe-nails
break and here
are the monuments of kings

St. George tends her blind father's grave
stretched out at your feet
like a cobbler hiring a hut
(24 instances noted)

O rose, take care —
take my ribs as a couch —
for her brother who is dying
we sold my sister's amulet

O organ of the nights,
four white rabbits
whose heads are like those of cauliflowers
shall strip (the leaves of) the myrtle

O for her sweet land and for those hills,
the foundation stone,
the captive bird,
the smell of a dead lion

I have no companion but you;
at the mention of your name
a thousand peacocks march in Asia

the rust is eating
a carafe full of red wine

she has been doing this for one or two years

and if you blow up the fire
it thinks that you belong to it

O mother of men,
I want to dance —

what is the matter?

In his hand is a book;
it may be the New Testament.

A thousand and one sighs for a draught from a jug.

Meticulously cutting his nails
he warms his eyes on our cheeks
prematurely

asking,
What use is the world?

2.

Barud,
faithful dog,
guardian of the orchard,
our lamp is failing

Hoarseness of autumn in its chest,
a parrot babbles on top of its cupboard,
a slipper gleams on its foot
like the seas of your eyes.

3.

Who scraped in the snow with her hands
saw fortunes; digs in the ashes,
a sky filled with perfumes

Decay has set in on
that dark blue and splendid iris;
I should not exchange this mill of ours
for the world.

4.

Wild mint
outside the house

no one knows what he wants to say
(35 instances noted)

5.

Never again shall we listen to the green curtains,
the orange peel old and blotchy

In my land is the porphyry —
I search this world for you.

The land of the lightning —
the world searches itself for you.

A veil of locusts —
the world goes round and round.

A pool of wine —
it is all pools of tar.

At the end of that garden
he spits red blood
on the rugs.

Wrapped in black headdresses
the white butterflies fly
in a temple that has collapsed on itself.

Like crystal in the moonlight
the carcass of a mule
full of acorns stained by red wine,
parsley and lettuce,
early red roses making the stones of the houses weep.

No bee remains in the hive.
A crow is swallowing the corpse.
Coming from the land of Persia:

no sweet girl, no songs, and no wine.
To build castles in order to warm you,
a thrush is building a nest in the woodwork of a coffin.

6.

On the day that we were created
the swords turned pale.

The scents of our clothing exhalations
of pistacchios and hazelnuts.

Your brown body
a worn and faded rug
dazzling with its diamonds.

It may be that it occurs to the world to moan.

A rose seller sold this Paradise at a loss.
Falsehood had laid its eggs —
between you and me.

7.

A parrot babbles
her hoop still clatters in the mist

wood of coffins
from the gold dust of your body

thus you leave the world.

Here is an abandoned bell.
Why this weariness, this trout?

It snows wine.
July is drowning.

Time Words

Just-in-time systems   9
Women — Time management   7
Time-series analysis   3
Time — Fiction   29
Time travel — History — 20th century   1
Time — Systems and standards — United States   2
March of time (Motion picture)   1
Powell, Anthony, 1905– Dance to the music of time   1
Time travel   5
     see also: Fourth dimension   12
Part-time employment   5
     see also: Supplementary employment   3
Time — Systems and standards   9
     see also: Daylight saving   1
     see also: Railroads — Time standards   1
Railroads — Time standards   1
Part-time employment — Oregon — Portland   1
Time — Systems and standards — Canada   1
Plants, Flowering of — North America — Flowering time   1
Equal time rule (Broadcasting) — United States — History   1
Time line (Computer file)   1
Time — Systems and standards — Canada — Handbooks,
    manuals, etc.   1
Time — Systems and standards — Mexico — Handbooks,
    manuals, etc.   1
Time — Systems and standards — United States —
    Handbooks, manuals, etc.   1
Time — Systems and standards — Handbooks, manuals, etc.
    1
Time — Juvenile poetry   2
Time management — Juvenile literature   1
Executives — Time management   6
Time — Poetry   3
Time — Philosophy   4
Time — Social aspects   5
Time — Political aspects   1
Time perception   8
Time in music   2
     see also: Musical meter and rhythm   29

Time (Law) — Oregon   1
Time, inc. — History   2
Time in literature   5
        see also: Future in literature   2
Businessmen — Time management   1
Time — Study and teaching (Elementary)   1
Space and time — History   2
Space and time — Juvenile literature   1
Time — Encyclopedias   1
Time — Religious aspects — Christianity   3
Time management — Philosophy   1
Parents — Time management   2
Children — Time management   1
Time — Systems and standards — United States — History
        1
Space and time in literature   2
Space and time in language   1
Time — Social aspects — Rome   1
Real-time data processing   4
        see also: Internet Relay Chat   2
        see also: Online chat groups   6
Time study   4
        see also: Motion study   5
Time measurements — Tables   2
Time — Systems and standards — United States — Tables   2
Space and time — Popular works   4
Homemakers — Time management   3
Planting time   3
Time measurements — Juvenile literature   1
White collar workers — Time management   1
Mothers — Time management   1
Geological time — Study and teaching — History   1
Time reversal   3
Time, inc. — Trials, litigation, etc.   1
School children — Time management   1
Time — Conversion tables   1
Fontaine, Robert Louis. Happy time   1
Time — Systems and standards — History   2

Time management — Computer programs   33
Space and time   53
        see also: Hyperspace   6
        see also: Personal space   12
        see also: Relativity (Physics)   63
        see also: Time reversal   3
        see also: Time travel   5
Time in art   1
Bagley, Clarence, 1843–1932. History of Seattle from the
    earliest settlement to the present time. — Indexes   1
College students — United States — Time management   3
Working mothers — Time management — United States   2
Russia — History — Time of Troubles, 1598–1613   1
Mothers — Time management — United States   3
Women — Time management — United States   4
Housewives — Time management — United States   1
Family — Time management — United States   5
Sports illustrated (Time, inc.) — Indexes   1
Parents — Time management — United States   1
Time perspective   1
Professional employees — Time management — United
    States   1
Prime Time (Ship)   1
Teachers — Time management — United States   1
Time pressure — United States   1
Hawking, S. W. (Stephen W.) Brief history of time   2
Parenting, Part-time   5
        see also: Single parents   8
Time measurements — History   2
Time — Interactive multimedia   1
Harvesting time — United States — Juvenile literature   1
Time — Systems and standards — Maps   6
Time perception — Cross-cultural studies   1
Jordan, Robert, 1948– Wheel of time. — Handbooks, manuals,
    etc.   1
Jordan, Robert, 1948– Wheel of time. — Illustrations   1
Space and time — Juvenile fiction   3
Part-time employment — United States — Statistics   1
Part-time farming — United States   1

Planting time — England — Juvenile literature   1
Time — Stories   1
Time travel in literature   4
Planting time — United States — Statistics   1
Harvesting time — United States — Statistics   1
Time travel — Drama   5
Students, Part-time — United States — Statistics   1
Students — Time management — United States   1
Time travel — Miscellanea   1
Family — Time management   2
Time management — Interactive multimedia   1
Engineers — Time management   1
Reaction time — Testing   1
Time — History   3
Time travel — Popular works   2
Time — Psychological aspects — Popular works   4
Time — Social aspects — Popular works   4
Space and time — Juvenile fiction — Sound recordings   1
Time — Exhibitions   1
Space and time — Interactive multimedia   1
Time pressure   2
Just-in-time systems — Accounting   1
Space and time in art   1
Space and time — Juvenile films   1
Time travel — Comic books, strips, etc.   1
Time — Religious aspects   1
Tippett, Michael, 1905– Child of our time   1
College teachers, Part-time — Training of — United States   1
Women — Time management — Religious aspects   1
Time — Study and teaching (Primary) — Interactive
        multimedia   1
Time — Systems and standards — Soviet Union — Maps   1
Students, Part-time   1
Students — Time management — Handbooks, manuals,
        etc.   1
Death — Time of   1
Time travel — Juvenile films   1
Time — Economic aspects   1

Public defenders — Time management — United States — States   1
Time mangerment   1
Equal time rule (Broadcasting) — United States   1
Time (Theology) — Comparative studies   1
Time — Social aspects — History   1
Space and time — Religious aspects — Catholic Church   2
Old-time music   13
Time-of-flight mass spectrometry — United States   1
Time in art — Exhibitions   1
Time perception — Exhibitions   1
AOL Time Warner   1
Time Warner   1
Businesspeople — Time management   1
Time dilatation   1
Time — Juvenile films   3
Time travel — Juvenile fiction   2
Time travel — Fiction — Juvenile sound recordings   1
Part-time farming   1
Real-time programming   2
College students — Time management   1
Time capsules — History — Juvenile literature   1
Time capsules   1
Time — Systems and standards — Law and legislation — United States   1
Time capsules — Drama   1
Time measurements — Exhibitions   1
Time management — United States — Case studies   1
Just-in-time manufacturing   0
    see: Just-in-time systems   9
Hours (Time)   0
    see: Chronology   5
    see: Horology   4
    see: Sundials   14
    see: Time   54
Space and time as a theme in literature   0
    see: Space and time in literature   2
Reversal, Time   0
    see: Time reversal   3

Time meters   0
     see: Chronometers   4
Time-limited counseling   0
     see: Short-term counseling   1
Time, Geological   0
     see: Geological time   8
Time-limited psychotherapy   0
     see: Brief psychotherapy   5
Analysis of time series   0
     see: Time-series analysis   3
Allocation of time   0
     see: Time Management   107
Budgets, Time   0
     see: Time Management   107
Personal time management   0
     see: Time Management   107
Time — Management   0
     see: Time Management   107
Time — Organization   0
     see: Time Management   107
Time — Use of   0
     see: Time Management   107
Time allocation   0
     see: Time Management   107
Time budgets   0
     see: Time Management   107
Time use   0
     see: Time Management   107
Use of time   0
     see: Time Management   107
Time and space   0
     see: Space and time   53
Quick time   0
     see: QuickTime   5
Time — Perception   0
     see: Time perception   8
Time, Cognition of   0
     see: Time perception   8
Time estimation   0

NEG

The bell is in the tower.
The bell is ringing.

Seeing is believing.
The car passing is John's.

The soldier will shoot to kill.
He can golf well.

Aaron is sleeping.
The lake has frozen over.
The lady was helped across the street.
Margaret will have forgotten by now.

Mexicans are here.
The fiesta will be tomorrow.

Father took us to Mexico.
They left whom in Mexico?

They speak the Spanish language.
They married the Indian women.

Most become citizens.
The Mexicans remained friends.

Mexicans seem interested.
The peppers taste hot.
The peppers remain hot.

A blue stone is valuable.
That material was left by mistake.
John is swimming in his pool.
Herbert Hoover had reason to be concerned.

Daniel bought a pumpkin — Illinois
is a large state, he drank his coffee.
Each house burned to the ground.
Patricia sold that china vase —

She wrote those song poems, my sons whispered.
Its color is green.

Soldiers built the bridges.
How many are there?

Knowledge is power.
How much is there?

Arithmetic was his favorite subject.
Snow covered the ground.
Discouragement came often.

Many had no shoes.
The war was finally won.

The book sleeps.
My window will rest today.

Money was a problem.
The war in Vietnam was his chief problem.

Blood is dripping.
Crowds bother me.

I gave her a picture.
She gave me one, too.

The semester draws to an end.
Soldiers fight in the jungles.

Most become citizens.
They appear happy.
Margaret seems intelligent.

Must many work outside?
Has Robert raised his hand?
Is the plane diving?

Are Mexicans here?
Do frogs sleep in winter?

The land is very different.
Swimmers are graceful.
Mexicans are here.
We have our language problems.
Some professionals are here.
Sports everywhere draw many people.
Sailboats are on sale.
We saw sails of many sizes blowing in the breeze.

We elected Timothy reporter.
He urged the crowd to leave.
The men required him to enroll.
The mother named the boy Moses.

George went to the library to plan for his trip.
The same was delayed a week in order for us to learn the rules.

The man swimming in the lake screamed.
I signed the paper taken by the doctor.

Mexicans are working where Jim works.
That was the reason why we waited.

First to Last

Now perhaps you will think that I am just lying to you, and maybe you will even think that Luther really wanted to get rid of the Jew kid so's we would oney have two ways to split instead of three, but you know, Mr. Breckenridge, guys like me can't never get away with bull like that to big-league lawyers like yourself, so you can just taken my word for it Fort didn't really mean to hurt the Jew kid a-tall, and that's the truth so help me. Late this afternoon she moved out of the old place into the new one. I woke up shaking, alone in my room. There is a certain shade of red brick — a dark, almost melodious red, sombre and riddled with blue — that is my childhood in St. Louis. I walked around outside and thought about it.

For several years, Mrs. H. T. Miller had lived alone in a pleasant apartment (two rooms with kitchenette) in a remodeled brownstone near the East River. Rain threatens. It didn't come all at once. The machine levelled off and settled on the aerodrome. She paused at the top of the staircase. The last letter I had from Harold was from Naples. Peter Morton woke with a start to face the first light. Everybody was drunk.

The stained, squashed cigaret hanging from Red's tight lips glowed, a tiny spark in the yellow glare that spilled from the enameled reflector at the ceiling. Mrs. Wilson was just taking the gingerbread out of the oven when she heard Johnny outside talking to someone. Neil's mother, Mrs. Campbell, sits on her lawn chair behind a card table outside the food co-op. Professor Barry Pennywither sat in a cold, shadowy garret and stared at the table in front of him, on which lay a book and a breadcrust. The farmer paid his labourers once a month, at sundown.

She could not bear to hurt her husband. She came in to the living room, her music satchel plopping against her winter-stockinged legs and her other arm weighted down with school books, and stood for a moment listening to the sounds from the studio. Inside, out of the rain, the lunch wagon was hot and sticky. Maurice Rosenfeld was conscious of himself as he took the key from his pocket and inserted it into the door of his small apartment. Previously, when I began to write this tale, I set out by saying that Mlle. Claude was a whore. Mr. Torrance had not slept well. It was early afternoon when Swan reached the brink of the hill that sloped down to town.

Old Dudley folded into the chair he was gradually molding to his own shape and looked out the window fifteen feet away into another window framed by blackened red brick. I was popular in certain circles, says Aunt Rose. Mr. Wheelock was clipping the hedge. Suddenly people began to disappear. Horizontally wakeful amid universal widths, practising laughter and mirth, satire, the end of all, of Rome and yes of Babylon, clenched teeth, remembrance, much warmth volcanic, the streets of Paris, the plains of Jericho, much gliding as of reptile in abstraction, a gallery of watercolors, the sea and the fish with eyes, symphony, a table in the corner of the Eiffel Tower, jazz at the opera house, alarm clock and the tap-dancing of doom, conversation with a tree, the river Nile, Cadillac coupe to Kansas, the roar of Dostoyevsky, and the dark sun. "You ought to wear a vest," his wife said, "and that's your fourth drink and it's only eight o'clock."

I am Gimpel the fool. She was a handsome baby, as babies go — a nice shade of red, with tiny black curls all over her head and the long fingers of a pianist or surgeon. You may have heard of Samuel Cramer, half poet, half journalist, who had to do with a dancer called the Fanfarlo. Except for the concluding words of this biography, Jake Fanner's longest speech was made in a cook shack near Caddo. It was close to five-thiry when he rang the Lutzes' doorbell.

Let me begin by saying that I don't know any more about where Professor Arthur Barnhouse is hiding than anyone else does. "To hell with dying," my father would say. R. J. Bowman, who for fourteen years had traveled for a shoe company through Mississippi, drove his Ford along a rutted dirt path. Hushed were the streets of many peopled Thebes.

Only her beautiful dead body remained for the hands of the mob. But nobody heard it. The man on the high old-fashioned bed with the quilt coverlet and the flowing white beard had been my first love. Good-by.

He glanced at the label, which read "Chateau Mouton-Rothschild 1937." "It's the seat o' my pants!" I was right, for presently, by the mute flashes of summer lightning we watched him ride the Zambesi away from us, among the rocks that look like crocodiles and the crocodiles that look like rocks. "Da!"

God be praised: there even Gimpel cannot be deceived. "The bastard!" he said, and lay back on his pillow to brood. The earth circled away, and knowing that he did so, he turned his lost face to the empty sky and became dreamless, unalive, perfect. But then Sydney turned and saw the old man moving away under the oak trees, and he broke for the sidewalk, crying, "Mister, Mister Man, please come back —" but before he could reach the sidewalk, the big black hearse, like an angry whale, came charging down the left side of the road to be first in the funeral line, and it crushed the boy to the ground, like feet crush acorns, and it shattered forever his thin glass voice. "Such a pretty little picture!"

Hug mama, tell her from Aunt Rose, goodbye and good luck. "I only tell people once," the man said and left the window. You just come on over anytime you want." He had one left, caught between his fingers, but he did not want it; it was not ripe. We ought to get out of this filthy hole and live somewhere in the sunshine, a room with a balcony overlooking a river, birds, flowers, life streaming by, just she and me and nothing else. "Tonight I will eat chopmeat." "By God, this is the happiest moment of my life."

Dragging her books and satchel she stumbled down the stone steps, turned in the wrong direction, and hurried down the street that had become confused with noise and bicycles and the games of other children. But no farther. He listened as he spoke, to hear how it would sound when he said it again, telling how he had shot blind into the grunting, invisible herd. It was April in Paris, and on the banks of the river the chestnuts were in bloom. Later, the plane makes a slow circle over New York City, and on it two men hold hands, eyes closed, and breathe in unison. "After *you*, my dear Alphonse."

It was bedtime. When they fired the first volley he was sitting down in the water with his head on his knees. And Agnes began to cry. His brain, too young to realize the full paradox, wondered with an obscure self-pity why it was that the pulse of his brother's fear went on and on, when Francis was now where he had always been told there was no more terror and no more darkness. I think he knows that I understand him and love him: at all events it comforts me to think so.

"Damn!" "Hello, you chaps." It will be time for Brahms and the great dry winds. The gutter water rushed over his feet, swirled frothing into a great whirlpool at the drain on the corner and rushed down to the center of the earth. "Hello," said Miriam. I didn't think I'd be that lucky, though, because I am too much a saga of a certain type of person: fuzzy blackness, impractical meditations and repressed desires.

Love him, you damn fool, love him. I got no story, Ma, I said. For the time being I have won. So help me.

TIMES OF DAY

At   to

Along

Often

By the way

Whom

Across   through

Sometimes

Below   down   downstairs

Store

Bee

Open

Lawyer

April

To open

Grandmother

Grandfather

Plenty

Dull

Accident

Action

Oil

Accept

About

Advise

Remember

Active

Action

Act

Ahead

Besides

Inside

Guess

Decorate

Adult

Warn

Airport

Hobby

Fond

Sorry

Lucky

Africa

Outside

Catch

August

Thank

Water

Sharp

Hole

Drown

Now

Save

Air

Beside

At least

Praise

Wire

Album

Reach

Village

Be glad

Cheerful   merry

Joy

German

Germany

Alphabet

Pin

Carpet

Anything   something

Cotton

Anybody   somebody

Ever

Any   some

Feed

Department store

Lunch

Around

Speaker

High   tall

Pupil

Lift

There

Kind

Love

Yellow

Both

America

American

Friend

Friendship

Friendly

Master

Love

Wide

Walk

Angle

Ring

Animal

Courage

Before

Announce

Add

Year

Appear

Aside

Hardly

Nickname

Learn

Hurry

Press

That

That

Those

Here

Tree

Bow

Rainbow

Area

Sand

Closet

Start

Dash

Above   up   upstairs

Rice

Art

Artist

Elevator

Set

So

As soon

Asia

Seat

Attend

Sunny

Matter   topic

To attack

Attack

Tie

Crowded

Atlantic

Charming

Attract

Back

Even

Still

Though

Golden

Absent

Bus

Avenue

Adventure

Ashamed

Airplane

Jet

Notice

Yesterday

Help

Roof

Sugar

Lily

Blue

To dance

Dance

Drop

Low

Balance

Ball

Basketball

Bank   bench

Band

Flag

Bath

Cheap

Barber

Boat

Sweep

Belly

Base

Enough   quite

Battle

Beat

Trunk

Drink

Baseball

Beauty

Lovely

To kiss

Kiss

Library

Bicycle

Well

Welcome

Blank   white

Block

Mouth

Wedding

Ticket

Bag   purse

Pocket

Pocketbook

Kindness

Beautiful

Forest   wood

Boots

Bottle

Button

Brave

Arm

Bright

Shine

Joke

Rough

Fine   good   ok

Ox

Gentleman

Horse

Cabin

Head

Each

Chain

Fall

Coffee

Box   case

Socks

Calendar

Hot

Heat

Street

Bed

Camera

Change   exchange

Change

Road

Shirt

Camp

Bell

Farmer

Country field

Song

Tired

Singer

Sing

Capital

Captain

Face

Character

Coal

Meat

Expensive

Race

Letter

Home   house

Marry

Almost   nearly

Case

Castle

Fourteen

Cause

Dig

Hunting

Celebrate

Supper

Central

Center

Brush

Near

By

Pig

Cherry

Zero

Close   shut

Lock

Basket

Heaven   sky

Science

Scientist

Hundred

Certainly

Certain

Five

Fifty

Movie

Ribbon   tape

Belt

Circus

Circle

Swan

City

Citizen

Clearly

Clear

Class   classroom   kind

Club

Kitchen

To cook

Cook

Car

Rocket

Tail

Collect

College

Anger

Hang

Hill

Lay

Color

Begin

Eat

Merchant

Trade

Food

Dinner   meal

Beginning   start

As   since

How

Comfortable

Company

Pity

Fully

Composition

Shopping

Buy

Common

With

Concert

Contest

Condition

Lead

Rabbit

Agree

Know

Knowledge

Get

Advice

Build

Count   tell

Watch

Reply

Continent

Continue

Against

105

Control

Conversation

Cup

Copy

Heart

Tie

Chorus

Crown

Correct

Runner

Mail   post

Run

Stream

Cut

Polite

Curtain

Short

Thing

Crop   harvest

Sew

Coast

To cost

Cost

Custom

Create

Grow

Believe

Cream

Maid

Servant

Cross

Notebook

Picture   square

Which

When

How much

Forty

Fourth   quarter   room

Bathroom

Four

Cover

To cover

Cuckoo

Spoon

Knife

Neck

Bill

Rope

Leather

Body

Crow

Cave

Care

Careful

Mind   take care

Culture

Top

Birthday

Course

Girl

Boy

Tiny

Little   small

Fun   joke

Driver

Lady

Give

Kick

Turn

From   of

Whose

Suddenly

Spare

Anyway

Under

Duty   must   should

Must

Homework

Weak

Decide

Tenth

Say

Finger

Leave   let

In front

Thin

Delicious

Dentist

Inside

Within

Apartment

Clerk

Sport

Law   right   strength

Waste

Breakfast

Rest

Discover

Careless

Since

Of course

Land

Desert

Slowly

Fair

Wake

Awake

Afterwards

After

After all

Behind

Day

Holiday

Daily   diary

Draw

Dictionary

December

Nineteen

Eighteen

Sixteen

Seventeen

Tooth

Teeth

Ten

Difference

Different

Difficult   hard

Difficulty

Worth

Hard

Money

God

Direction

Direct

Record

Speech

Discussion

Discuss

To design

Design

Shoot

Distance

Different

Bend

Double

Twelve

Dozen

Doctor

Dollar

Address

Sunday

Where

Asleep

Sleep

Two

Twice

Drama

Drugstore

Shower

Doubt

Candy   sweet

Twelfth

During

Hard

Lie

Age

Building

Education

Example

Exercise

Army

The

He

Electricity

Electric

Elephant

She

They

It

They

Exciting

Pack

Sandwich

Begin

Job

Push

At   in   into

Abroad

Instead

At once

Everywhere

Indeed

Loudly

Charm

Find   meet

Enemy

Energy

January

Illness

Nurse

Sick

Wipe

Angry

Try

Show   teach

Understand

Whole

Then

Entrance

Enter

Among   between

Interview

Send

Age

Team

Mistake

Are

Is

That

Stair

Scene   stage

Hide

Spell   write

Writer

Desk

Listen to

School

That

That

Space

Sword

Back

Spain

Spanish

Special

Especially

Sort

Mirror

Hope

Expect   hope   wait

Spirit

Wife

Ski

Corner

This

Is

Tonight

Season   station

State

Are

Stamp

Farm

Pond

Be

These

Are

Height

East   this

Style

These

Am

Narrow

Star

Student

Study

Stupid

Europe

European

Exactly

Examination

Excellent

Except

Picnic   tour

Excuse

Success

Experience

To experience

Explain

Express

Spread

Foreign   foreigner

Wonder

Strange   strange

Party

Fix

End

Finally

Fine   nice

Arrow

Loose

Flower

Bloom

Vase

Float

Flow

Bottom

Form   shape

Fortune   match

Photo   picture

Photograph

Fail

French

France

Front

Fresh   cool

Bean

Cold

Fruit

Fire

Strong

Power

Smoke

Gun

Shoot

Football   soccer

Future

Hen

Cock

Win

Gas

Spend

Cat

General

Generally

People

Gentle

Gently

Knock   strike

Fat

Cap

Enjoy

Funny

Grade

Big   great   large

Greatly

Barn

Greece

Gray

Shout

Thick

Group

Glove

Handsome

Keep

War

Able

Ability

Habit

Speak   talk

Do   make

Become

Song

Attempted   imagined

Subway

Walking

Waiting

Similar

Substitution

Surprise

About   toward

Farm

Find

Be

Hungry

Until

Till

Fact

Sister

Brother

Tool

Boil

Ice

Grass

Iron

Daughter

Son

History   story

Home

Leaf   sheet

Hello

Man

Men

Shoulder

Deep

Honor

Honest

Hour

Ant

Hospital

Hotel

Today

Bone

Guest

Egg

Escape

Human

Wet

Smoke

Sink

Idea

Ideal

Language

Church

Imagine

Magnet

Important

Amount

Impossible

Print

To print

Tax

Bow

Even

Report

Information

Engineer

England

English

Intend

Interest

Interesting

Be interested

International

Flood

Invention

Invent

Inventor

Winter

Invitation

To invite

Go

Island

Left

Soap

Pull

Japan

Japanese

Garden

Zoo

Cage

Jazz

Chief

Young

Thursday

Player

Play

Toy

July

June   join

Close

Together

Fair

Judge

Kilogram

Her

It

The

Lip

Side

Bark

Brick

Rubber

Lake

Tear

Lamp

Wool

Throw

Dash   rush

Pencil

Leader

Light

Limit

Lemon

Clean   pretty   line

List

Clever

Ready

Butterfly

On a Tuesday in March, MORE, MOST, and RATHER MORE
OR LESS LATER killed mathematics. In May, MORE, the
senior, said, "Me, I'm stocking medicine in stockings,
and on the average, in the middle, at noon, say, when the
cheek is best, better than a memory —" MOST, the junior,
interrupted, "— least, less than the next message, or the
mind lies!" In the market, a month later, a table at the Inn
was metal for less than a meter. The same mystery had half
the meeting (fashion models with modern manners are
trouble) the moment the coin was given to the monkey in
the mountains. Girl and boy crowd many, much furniture
in the Spring. Death is dead. A woman in women is a world,
doll wrist, museum music, and the she-musician is very all
right but waiting born. A nation is only a national habit,
none when nothing interferes with swimming. Nobody's
card is orange. The necessary need is to need business, black
baby nor nest but fog snow child, children level not cannot
in the night find a name north of us, we note notice news
novels the ninth of the ninetieth November is a cloud in a
cloudy way our ninth new number never (or never) ocean.
And then idle. On the Eighth of October busy. The Office
of Hearing, eyes waved from smell to smell, forgetting
eleven chance sentences. The speaker ordered ordinary ears
an organ, proud shore of gold spelling swinging darkness
like the bear in Autumn. Fall again another else other sheep
find no pacific father, parent to pay the page country, straw
bird a word palace bats stuck with bread. It is a screen.
The pair for forever, parade to stop umbrellas to stop
seeming walls, coupling parks, part game, game matched
in the past. Not long ago a passenger was a pass, a walk a
step, a potato a skate. Peace a piece — fight film. Danger
dangerous, hair thought. Think a rock; worse, worst, lose
newspaper period. The pearl of my person belongs to the
heavy fishing, fish weight fish piano, pick foot stone skin.
Leg foot piece paint. The painter of paint is a picture of
a pipe. The pyramids are pools, blackboards of pleasure.

The plan plans the planet flat, plants a silver platform, the poor are few, a little are able and can and may be the last poem of the police post-well a practiced practice and the price is a question. Ask.

NOTES

Franz Kamin was an experimental composer, pianist, author, and teacher active in Bloomington, New York City, the Hudson Valley, and St. Paul. His example and encouragement were indispensable to scores of students and friends, and his generosity and courage continue to inspire my work.

"Statements on Doing Nothing" appears in *Ann Margret Loves You and Other Psychotopological Diversions* (Barrytown, NY: Station Hill, 1980); his other books, also from Station Hill, include the novel *Scribble Death* and the forthcoming *Theory of Angels*.

Conduction

This montage was written in response to the work of visual artist Anna Hepler, and first appeared in a somewhat different form in the exhibition catalogue *Conduit* (Seoul: Modular Unit Design, 2000). Quoted passages (set in italics) are keyed to their sources via the list that follows.

In addition, the thoughts and works of friends and others found their way into my words through paraphrase, reference, and regard. Thus I offer my oblique but sincere acknowledgments to Laurie Durante, Gene Frumkin, Joseph Krupczynski, Marge Piercy, John Cage, Ruth Bernhard, Mauricio Alejo, anonymous authors of computer architecture manuals, Mahler's Ninth Symphony, Los Monroy, and the Templo Mayor in Mexico City.

AH1   Anna Hepler, interview with Oliver Broudy

AH2   Anna Hepler, letter to the author

BG   Bruce Boone & Robert Gluck, *La Fontaine* (San Francisco: Black Star, 1981)

ED   *The Poems of Emily Dickinson* (#1779), edited by
        R.W. Franklin (Cambridge, MA: Belknap, 1998)

FK1   Franz Kamin, "Yellow Room," *Ann Margret Loves
        You and Other Psychotopological Diversions*
        (Barrytown, NY: Station Hill, 1980)

FK2   Franz Kamin, *Scribble Death* (Barrytown, NY:
        Station Hill, 1986)

FM   Friederike Mayröcker, *with each clouded peak,*
        translated by Rosmarie Waldrop & Harriett Watts
        (Los Angeles: Sun & Moon, 1998)

FN   Friedrich Nietzsche, *On the Advantage and
        Disadvantage of History for Life*, translated by
        Peter Preuss (Indianapolis: Hackett, 1980)

FT   Transcribed from a wall painting at Salon
        Familiar "Tiburon," Veracruz, Mexico, January
        2000

GB   Gregory Bateson, "Men Are Grass: Metaphor and
        the World of Mental Process," *A Sacred Unity:
        Further Steps to an Ecology of Mind* (New York:
        Harper Collins, 1991)

JB   John Berger, "Drawn to that moment," *The Sense
        of Sight*, edited by Lloyd Spencer (New York:
        Pantheon, 1985)

JC1   John Cage, "The Future of Music," *Empty Words*
        (Middletown, CT: Wesleyan University Press,
        1979)

JC2   Julio Cortázar, "House Taken Over," *End of the
        Game and Other Stories*, translated by Paul
        Blackburn (New York: Pantheon, 1967)

JG   Johann Wolfgang von Goethe, "Prologue in the
        Theater," *Faust* Part I, translated by Randall Jarrell
        (New York: Farrar, Straus, & Giroux, 1976)

JL1   Jaron Lanier, "You Can't Argue with a Zombie,"
        Journal of Consciousness Studies, Vol. 2, No. 4,
        1995

JL2   Jaron Lanier, "The Eternal Now," *Forbes ASAP*, February 22, 1999

MC   Meng Chiao, "Autumn Thoughts, I," *The Late Poems of Meng Chiao*, translated by David Hinton (Princeton, NJ: Princeton University Press, 1996)

MP   Maxfield Parrish, from a letter referring to the blank canvas of what was to become the painting *Daybreak*, basis for the fabulously popular print

NB   Nadia Boulanger, in *Mademoiselle: Conversations with Nadia Boulanger* by Bruno Monsaingeon, translated by Robyn Marsack (Boston: Northeastern University Press, 1988)

OD   Brian O'Doherty, "Rauschenberg and the Vernacular Glance," *Art in America* 61, Sept–Oct 1973

OH   Frank O'Hara, introduction to *Dancers, Buildings, and People in the Street* by Edwin Denby (New York: Horizon, 1965)

PV   Paul Valéry, "My Bust," *Degas, Manet, Morisot*, translated by David Paul (New York: Pantheon, 1960)

RH   Robert Hughes, *The Shock of the New* (New York: Knopf, 1980)

RM   Eric Nagourney, "Roger A. Morse, Expert on Bees' Sweet Science, Dies at 72," *New York Times*, May 21, 2000

RR   Robert Rauschenberg, in *Off the Wall: Robert Rauschenberg and the Art of Our Time* by Calvin Tomkins (New York: Penguin, 1981)

SK   Stanley Klein, "Will Robots See?" in *Spatial Vision in Humans and Robots*, edited by Laurence Harris and Michael Jenkins (New York: Cambridge University Press, 1993)

Orbis Pictus

Orbis Sensualium Pictus, one of the first picture-books intended specifically for children, was published in 1658 by the Czech writer and teacher Jan Amos Komensky (John Amos Comenius), considered by some to be the father of modern education. The title *Orbis Pictus* has been adopted on many occasions since, particularly for book series that aspire to provide a pictorial guide to the world.

The first two sections of this ongoing project were written in the late 1980s, drawing on the delightful pocket-sized hardcover *Orbis Pictus* volumes issued in the 1960s by the Swiss publisher Hallwag. "Land Sought, Found, Claimed" mines volume 9, *Precious Stones* (as well as the words of Nelson Goodman and Gertrude Stein); "Ambulatory Windows" refracts volume 4, *The Stained Glass Windows at Chartres*.

Sources for the epigraphs:

Paul Valéry, "Fragment from 'On Poe's Eureka,'" translated by Malcolm Cowley, *Selected Writings* (New York: New Directions, 1950)

James Hillman, *Inter Views: Conversations with Laura Pozzo on Psychotherapy, Biography, Love, Soul, Dreams, Work, Imagination, and the State of the Culture* (New York: Harper & Row, 1983)

David Antin, "definitions for mendy," *Selected Poems 1963–1973* (Los Angeles: Sun & Moon, 1991)

"Lebanon"

This homage/travesty draws extensively from *The Poetic Vocabulary of Michel Trad: A Study in Lebanese Colloquial Poetry* by M. C. Lyons and E. I. Maalouf (Beirut: Librairie du Liban, 1968).

Michel Trad (1912–1998), whose poems were widely memorized (and served as lyrics for songs by Fairuz and others), worked for more than thirty years as an administrator in the Roman ruins of Baalbeck in the Bekaa valley.

"Time Words"

The result of a search for subject classifications that include the word "time," as represented in the Multnomah County (Oregon) Library online catalog in 2005.

"NEG"

Example sentences from *The New English Grammar*, Charles L. Thompson (Palo Alto, CA: Fearon, 1970).

"First to Last"

The first and last sentence from each of the stories in *First Fiction: An Anthology of the First Published Stories by Famous Writers*, edited by Kathy Kiernan and Michael M. Moore (Boston: Little, Brown, 1994).

Times of Day

Written in a ledger book in 1984 and forgotten for fifteen years, this piece was rediscovered and transcribed in 1999.

About the Author

David Abel is an editor and teacher in Portland, Oregon, and the proprietor of Passages Bookshop and The Text Garage.

He is the publisher (with Sam Lohmann) of the *Airfoil* chapbook series, and edits and produces the free broadside series *Envelope*. A founding member of the Spare Room reading series (now in its eleventh year) and the collaboration collective 13 Hats, he is also a Research Fellow of the Center for Art + Environment of the Nevada Museum of Art. As an interdisciplinary artist, he has devised numerous performance, film, theater, and intermedia projects with a wide range of co-conspirators. In 2011, he curated the international exhibition *Object Poems* for 23 Sandy Gallery in Portland.

His recent publications include the chapbooks *Tether* (Bare bone books), *Carrier* (c_L), *Commonly* (Airfoil), and *Black Valentine* (Chax), and the collaborative artist's books *While You Were In* and *Let Us Repair* (disposable books, with Leo & Anna Daedalus).

About Chax Press

Chax Press has been publishing books in Tucson Arizona since 1984. Recent works include books by Norman Fischer, Samuel Ace & Maureen Seaton, Leslie Scalapino, Charles Olson, Mark Weiss, Drum Hadley, Andrew Levy, Rodney Phillips, fine letterpress chapbooks by Anne Waldman and Eileen Myles, and many more. We have published 139 books to date, and look forward to many more in the next several years. Please visit our web site at *chax.org*, and look for our books at the Small Press Distribution web site, *http://spdbooks.org*. Chax Press has received support from the Southwestern Foundation for Educational and Historical Preservation, the Tucson Pima Arts Council, the Arizona Commission on the Arts, and the National Endowment for the Arts, but the greatest part of our support comes from individual donors. To join our supporters, please visit our web donation page at *http://chax.org/donate.htm*.